I0419588

Self-Discipline: No More Excuses!

How To Gain Willpower and Self-Control

By

Michele Gilbert

<u>Visit My Amazon Author Page</u>

Dedicated to those who choose to stretch beyond their own limits and to seek a more abundant and fulfilling life.

Your thoughts are creative.

Michele Gilbert

My Free Gift To You!

As a way of saying thank you for downloading my book, I am willing to give you access to a selected group of readers who (every week or so) receive inspiring, life-changing kindle books at deep discounts, and sometimes even absolutely free.

Wouldn't it be great to get amazing Kindle offers delivered directly to your inbox?

Wouldn't it be great to be the first to know when I'm releasing new fresh and above all sharply discounted content?

But why would I so something like this?

Why would I offer my books at such a low price and even give them away for free when they took me countless hours to produce?

Simple.... because I want to spread the word!

For a few short days Amazon allows Kindle authors to promote their newly released books by offering them deeply discounted (up to 70% price discounts and even for free. This allows us to spread the word extremely quickly allowing users to download thousands and thousands of copies in a very short period of time.

Once the timeframe has passed, these books will revert back to their normal selling price. That's why you will benefit from being the first to know when they can be downloaded for free!

So are you ready to claim your weekly Kindle books?

You are just one click away! Follow the link below and sign up to start receiving awesome content

Thank you and Enjoy!

Table of contents

Introduction

I want to thank you and congratulate you for downloading my book, *"Self-Discipline : The Ultimate Beginners Guide.* This book contains proven steps and strategies to show you how self-discipline can help you live your ideal life. You will learn to better define what you want your ideal life to look like and how to use the power of self-discipline and willpower to achieve it.

It's easy to understand why some of us have come to regard the idea of "self-discipline" as something unpleasant, as a way of denying ourselves or by beating ourselves up physically with our demanding exercise regimens, with negative self-talk, by continuing to deprive ourselves of something we need or love. Fortunately, this has nothing to do with the practice of real self-discipline.

The word "discipline" is Latin word *disciplina,* meaning "teaching" or "learning" One who studied such knowledge, was known as a "disciple," which simply means "student."

Thanks again for downloading this book, I hope you enjoy it!

CHAPTER 1: Why Self-Disciple Is So Important

Learning to develop self-discipline is an amazing skill that everyone should consider. It's an important and very useful part of a life well lived. It's essential in every facet of your life, and even though people will acknowledge and agree with its importance, very few will do something to strengthen or act on it.

Most people believe self-discipline means being harsh or denying yourself of the things that you enjoy. They believe it is living in a limited, restrictive type lifestyle. Self-discipline actually means having or developing self-control. It is a sign of your powerful inner strength. With Self-discipline you develop the power to implement and stick to your decisions and follow them through to completion without changing your mind. It is one of the most important requirements for achieving your goals in every area of your life.

To begin on the road to self-discipline you must break bad habits. One of the main reasons that bad habits are so hard to break is what some researchers call "cognitive script". These are the unconscious and automatic thoughts that we have when we come across a familiar situation. They are based on previous experiences. They are familiar experiences that we have had many times before and become ingrained behaviors that we do without thinking. And those actions become habitual.

The good news is you can break bad habits or replace them with better, more powerful and positive ones.

Unfortunately, and this is the hard part. It takes time. The time to break a habit varies. Some studies show on average changing a bad habit and replacing it with a positive one can take anywhere from 18 -254 days depending on the habit and the person. But honestly, there is no "one size fits all."

Some people may think that self-discipline is being strong enough, tough enough or focused enough to resist all temptations. But I've discovered one of the best ways to become more disciplined is simply by helping yourself. You need to try to remove all temptations and distractions from the situations where you need to get task done.

Why is it that there are some people that seem to get so much done? How can they manage to publish a book or create a new work of art, while others will just sit around dreaming of things they want to accomplish. The secret to getting things done is walking the fine line between self-discipline and self-care.

So what commitments will you make to yourself? What goals are you going to begin to commit to?

Making a commitment to yourself to achieve a goal whether it is big or small, is the same as making a commitment to someone else. And there's no one to disappoint but you. You must learn to keep your commitments to others as well as yourself.

When you commit to achieving a goal, or a dream or to make a complete change in your life that may mean giving up something else. Maybe you don't go out with your friends as often or spend as much time with your family as you'd like. Or you don't join all the clubs you're interested in, or watch your favorite sports team on TV ...But that's just the way it is. That's just the way it has to be.

There can be no excuses. Making excuses is like giving up before you even begin. Keep your goals in sight and really commit to them—and to yourself— absolutely, no matter what.

What are you committed to? Write it down. Title it ..."My Commitment to Myself"

Put your goals on paper, see it clearly, and then get started.

CHAPTER 2: Describe Your Ideal Life And Then Go Out And Get It.

Do you really know what you want? What will make you happy and come alive? Your self-discipline journey can really be powerful if you start with self-discovery. Here are some ways to set you on the path.

Visualize your ideal life

Go somewhere and close your eyes and imagine what an ideal life looks like to you. Family? Children?
Where do you live?
Are you working? What hobbies light you up?
What is the first thing you do when you get up in the morning?
What does your day look like?
Who are your friends?

Prioritize

So now you have a list of things that you envision as part of an ideal life. Now let's prioritize it. The point is for you to focus your efforts. The truth is that we have a limited amount of time and energy. So get started today

Things not on the list

Look at your list and take some time to think about the things that were not included
New car?
New cell phone?
Expensive toys?

The point is to recognize some of the things that are currently a part of your life but are not a part of your ideal life. If you can recognize what those things are, you can decrease the amount of time and money you spend on them. This will give you more time and money for the things that matter.

Start taking action

Planning IS important, but we can spend all day dreaming and never get anywhere. At some point we have to start creating. With self-discipline we can begin to proceed.

Re-evaluate

Remember that your ideal life will always be an evolving dream. Life is always changing. You are always changing. There will be new and unexpected twists and turns. This means that this will be an ongoing process that will have to be re-evaluated from time to time.

CHAPTER 3: Self-Discipline And The Wealthiest People In The World

Do you think billionaires have self-disciple? You know the answer I'm sure. They are often laser focused and do not deviate until the job is done. If they can do it so can you.

Providing, of course, that money is important to you here is what the world's richest people do and how they practice self-discipline every single day. This is based on the Forbes World Billionaire list.

They have a routine.

Maintain a to-do list

Wake up 3+ hours before work

Listen to Audio books

Network 5+ hours or more a month

Read 30+ minutes each day

Love to read

Exercise 4 days a week

Teach good success habits to their children

Make their children volunteer 10+ hours a month

Encourage their children to read 2+ non-fiction books a month

They watch less than 1 hour a day of TV

Write down their goals

Focus on accomplishing a specific goal

Believe in lifelong educational self-improvement

Believe good habits create opportunity

Believe bad habits have a negative impact.

Pick a few and make it a part of your daily habits and see the difference it will make in your life. Besides what you will discover about yourself will be amazing.

CHAPTER 4: Self-Disciple And A Healthy Lifestyle

There is no one who can force you to eat right and exercise regularly, you must use self-discipline to get up off the couch and throw away whatever it is that you are eating. It's not easy, but you can improve self-discipline with practice.

Creating a plan with small, measurable goals can help you to maintain self-control which, in turn, can help you to get back on track if you have fallen off.

The Importance of Willpower

By exercising willpower it will give you the self-discipline you need to maintain a healthy lifestyle. When those temptations that pop up sometimes seem too powerful to ignore, you're not alone. Several surveys that have been conducted show that lack of willpower keeps most people from making changes in their lives, such as healthy eating and exercise. But the most important concept that must be understood is that willpower is a learned behavior. Let me repeat that. Willpower is a learned behavior!

The more often you try to resist temptation -- whether it's the urge to eat an unhealthy snack or to skip your evening run -- the stronger your willpower can become.

Setting Realistic Goals

The key to maintaining self-discipline is setting short and long-term goals that are attainable. If you try to exercise seven days a week that might not be realistic. However, maybe if you try to exercise four or five days a week that might be a more attainable goal. Short-term goals should be benchmarks that lead up to long-term goals. If you want to lose weight, set a six-month goal, break it down into smaller pieces, like losing one pound every two weeks. Reaching these smaller milestones can help to keep you motivated, which is another factor in maintaining your self-discipline.

Self-Care

This is often-ignored but so totally necessary, self-care is any action or behavior that helps us **to avoid triggering health concerns** (like increasing our risk for heart problems due to excess stress,) self-care benefits us by improving our mental and physical health with better self-esteem, discipline, less stress, and overall wellbeing.. Self-care is so important that it is an essential part of a healthy lifestyle as it keeps us healthy, happy, and more in-tune with our minds and bodies. Some experts suggest that we neglect self-care because it can be very **tough to make healthy changes and we don't have the self-discipline we need** to manage our stress in better ways. Self-care is also sometimes **mistaken for selfishness, narcissistic,** lazy, and over-indulgent behavior.

This might make us feel guilty for thinking we need to take a break to do something that could make us feel better. Ignoring our needs can also have some dangerous side effects: It makes us more susceptible tc getting sick and can make existing conditions worse—and don't forget the emotional toll of never taking a break.

CHAPTER 5: Self-Discipline and Self-Discovery

Writers

Most writers sit in their chair for hours, inspecting their work, blocking out the rest of the world with focused concentration. It is not easy. They are practicing self-discipline. I am sure that readers have no idea how many endless hours they toil away at their writings. It takes immense self-discipline to sit in that chair when they could be enjoying the sunshine and beautiful weather outside. Most times writers wait for "inspiration" to strike. And when it does, the story almost always is a great idea. The problem is seeing that idea through to completion, To get there, they need some good writing habits and self-discipline.

Actually there is really only one good writing habit and that is you must write constantly. According to Merriam-Webster, self-discipline is: correction or regulation of oneself for the sake of improvement. Writers like all other artists are constantly searching, digging, investigating for that one great idea for the sake of improvement.

Journaling

Journaling can be a powerful tool for self-growth and self-discovery. Using your journaling practice for self-improvement requires self-discipline as well as it can help you get focused on the things you want to achieve in your life. It can help you determine the steps you need to take to get you there -- and , of course, improve your self-discipline by providing a framework for getting things done!

Whatever it is you want to gain in your life, you can use your journal to make it happen, including:
- Secure a new job - or a new career! Write about it.
- Start a business Write about it.
- Manage your finances
- Achieve your financial goals
- Lose weight.. then keep a journal
- Learn something new.. Then write about it.
- Improve your relationships ...then put your feeling on paper.

If there is something you've been telling yourself you can't do like adhering to self-discipline then journaling can help you gain new perspective, change your thought patterns, develop inner strength and stop letting your inner critic stand in your way!

Gratitude

"Gratitude bestows reverence, allowing us to encounter everyday epiphanies, those transcendent moments of awe that change forever how we experience life and the world." —Sarah Ban Breathnach in *Simple Abundance*

Developing a self-discipline practice of gratitude is essential for us to grow. Perhaps thinking of gratitude as a spiritual discipline is a new idea for you. Growing and continuing in spiritually means that we need to continue to expand our thinking of what spiritual disciplines are. There is the discipline of surrender, the discipline of listening, the discipline of denying self, the discipline of waiting. And then there is the discipline of gratitude.

Meditation

There are so many ways and reasons that meditation improves self-discipline here are just a couple.

1. Meditation helps you to stay clear and in the moment.

There is nothing like instant gratification and that feeling we get from immediate results. Meditation helps us to understand our inner thoughts and the difference between wanting and needing. When we meditate we get clearer on our long term goals and help to make them that much stronger.

2. Meditation helps to activate the "will power" part of the brain.

There have been findings that showed that the "dorsolateral prefrontal cortex" is the section of the brain activated by people with high levels of willpower. Interestingly enough this is the same area of the brain that is particularly active during meditation, as evidenced by numerous research studies.

3. Meditation releases "feel good" chemicals in the brain.

There are chemicals, like dopamine and endorphins that are in the body/brain that when released make us feel amazing and almost "high" Meditation has been shown to elicit these same chemicals in a very natural and healthy way,

4. Meditation melts away the stress and anxiety.

Meditation has been proven to work even better than exercise to permanently reduce stress and anxiety levels within the body

CHAPTER 6: 10 Ways To Help Develop Willpower
1. Meditate

Meditation as the #1 way to increase willpower

2. Exercise

It's also been shown to improve our willpower

3. Accountability

The idea is that when we're left to our own devices, it's easy to come up with excuses not to do something. Get someone to hold you accountable.

4. Goals

What are your clear goals for yourself? They give you a clear direction in life and help you connect your daily actions to a greater purpose. Both purpose and clarity will jump start your willpower

5. Remove Temptations and Distractions

It is so important to figure out a system to bulletproof ourselves against all these distractions. Distractions are the ultimate time waster and dream killer. Willpower will put an end to that.

6. Do The Hardest First

Our willpower is at its highest at the beginning of the day, and progressively decreases as we go about our business.

7. Eliminate Unnecessary Decisions

Try to eliminate or minimize all unimportant tasks and preserve your brainpower for what truly matters.

Create Powerful Habits, Rituals and Routines

Creating rituals is a great way to remove needless decision-making from your day. Once something has been become a habit, you don't even have to think about it anymore. You do it without using any of your willpower.

Use The 5-Minute Rule

If you're struggling to get started on some work you have to do, or to start your daily meditation/workout, make the following deal with yourself that you will do it for just 5 minutes. I promise you, from my experience, once you get started you will do more than 5 minutes. It's just about getting started.

Go for 100% Commitment

If you really want to do something, commit to it 100%.

You'll waste a lot of willpower fighting with your inner voice.

But the moment have you that 100% commitment, it becomes easy. You don't have to think about it... you just do it!

CHAPTER 7: Quotes To Help Keep You Motivated

Self-discipline helps us to reach our goals and keeps our attitude high. Truthfully, discipline is the foundation of happiness and could be one of the most important requirements for success however you define it. These are a selection of quotes that contain proverbs and citations related to discipline, self-control, determination and willpower

Let them lead you... and hopefully motivate and inspire you...

"There are no short cuts to any place worth going."

— Beverly Sills

Keep away from people who belittle your ambitions. Small people always do that, but the really great make you feel that you, too, can become great."

— Mark Twain

"If we don't discipline ourselves, the world will do it for us."

— William Feather

"Mastering others is strength. Mastering yourself is true power."

— Lao Tzu

The first and best victory is to conquer self."

— Plato
Greek Philosopher

"I think the guys who are really controlling their emotions ... are going to win."

— Tiger Woods

"Rule your mind or it will rule you."

— Horace

"Leaders aren't born they are made. And they are made just like anything else, through hard work. And that's the price we'll have to pay to achieve that goal, or any goal."

— Vince Lombardi

"Success is a matter of understanding and religiously practicing specific, simple habits that always lead to success."

— Robert J. Ring

Conclusion

Self-discipline is an act of cultivation. It requires you to connect today's actions to tomorrow's results. There's a season for sowing a season for reaping. Self-discipline helps you know which is which ~Gary Ryan Blair

We all have dreams. But in order to make dreams come into reality, it takes an awful lot of determination, dedication, self-discipline, and effort ~Jesse Owens

It is better to conquer yourself than to win a thousand battles. Then the victory is yours. It cannot be taken from you, not by angels or by demons, heaven or hell ~Buddha

I have been meditating every day for the past 2 years, and it's the single-best habit I've developed to help me slow down the process and develop real clarity.

Before you go, I'd like to say thank you for purchasing my book.

I know you could have picked so many other books to read on overcoming rejection. But you took a chance on me.

So A Big thanks for downloading this book and reading it all the way to completion.

Now I would like to ask a _small_ favor.

Could you please take a minute or two to leave a review for this book on Amazon?

Click here

The feedback will help me continue to publish more kindle books that will help people to get better results in their lives.

And if you found it helpful in anyway then please let me know :-)

Preview of My New Book

Meditation For Beginners: How To Meditate For Lifelong Peace, Focus and Happiness

CHAPTER 1 - What is Meditation

I sit here trying to focus on my writing and my mind hums like a runaway train. My mind seems to be in a never ending race – running towards what, I don't know. But all I know is that I need to calm down and slow down. I indicated this to my friend recently and he suggested that that I engage in meditation. Meditation; I did not think it possible to meditate among all the noise and distractions that seem to permeate every fibre aspect of living. As the reader of this eBook, you may be having the same kind of thoughts. However, it is for this very reason this eBook has been written, to explore the practice of meditation and discover what is possible when we think not.

We are often burdened with the stresses of everyday living. It does not mean that it is all negative stress, for when you love, when your family is in harmony, or when your team is upbeat about the project it is working on at work, these are all positive actions. They also put some pressure on you for your time, commitment and involvement. In fact, these are happy times for you. There are, however, the negative stresses also that seem to overwhelm our every waking thought and make us feel out of control. But this is the stuff life is made of, and probably it is what makes the world go round. Just imagine this as a roller coaster ride, bumping and swinging you all over the place. Some things are even beyond our control, like sickness, death, loss of job, fears, the demands of family, and the need to take care of ourselves. For this we need a place of peace where we can conquer and tame the inner self, place brakes on the runaway train of our minds, and bring back balance and stability to mind and body.

Many times you may have seen persons engaged in the practice of yoga. They sit still, maybe with crossed legs and eyes closed, and may appear to be in deep concentration. It is as if they are "not here", and are very far away. They are engaged in meditation. Meditation is part of an old Buddhist tradition for one to control the mind, by bringing it into a state of consciousness and calm, relieving it from the clutter and the din of distractions that constantly seek its attention. You will find that although you have not made a conscious effort of it, you often are engaged in meditation. When you sit and watch the birds hopping from branch to branch or courting with each other, or at the sea shore you gaze across the horizon, or you view the green cascade of trees on the hills in quiet amazement, you are in meditation mode. It is only when you are "out" of that mode that you realize how far off your thoughts had gone. Once your mind is drawn to be one in concentration, it is meditation.

Singh (2015) describes meditation as getting in touch and communicating with our inner self. Meditation is you communicating with you. It is the cleansing of the mind, being viewed in the same way as the act of the cleansing of the body. The Meditation Society of America (2014) describes meditation as a three step process. I like the fact that meditation is learning to use the mind to develop the skill of being mindfully aware of what gets in there, without judgement, and accepting it with compassion and patience. It means that the meditative mind accepts that there are negative things that will enter the mind. However, it recognizes it, accepts it, understands what is happening and deals with it in a positive and sympathetic manner. In this way, the negative things cannot hurt you because your mind controls them.

Meditation is all about a positive response to your inner thoughts and gaining insight. The word meditation is said to come from the Latin words *meditari,* which means to think or dwell upon or to exercise the mind, and *mederi,* which means to heal. In Sanskrit, meditation means wisdom. When you meditate you emerge a wiser person. Your way is clearer.

Use of Breath in Meditation

The most basic element of most forms of meditation is the use of breath. Breath is used to focus the attention of the thoughts of the mind with the realization that our thoughts are easily diverted from one place to the other. The meditation technique focuses concentration on the flow of breath through the nose, by altering the depth, rate or pattern of its inflow and outflow to reach a meditative state. The breath is used to develop mindfulness in the person and is also used to transcend different levels of meditation for ecstasy and bliss.

Use of Mantras

Another element of meditation is the use of mantras or sounds. Mantras can involve the hum or repetition of words (chant) that represent the values with which society holds dear, such as Love, Truth and God. Simple rhythmic sounds are used to break into the concentration of the mind and help to point the thoughts towards a particular object. It also sets the mood for the mind to accept new things. An example of a mantra in Kundalini meditation is "Sat Nam", meaning "Truth is my Identity". According to Singh, chanting this mantra awakens the soul.

CHAPTER 2 - Misconceptions about Meditation

Many times you have come across persons to whom when you mention the practice of meditation, they will say "Oh, I've tried it before, but it did not work for me". Or, you may hear one say, "I failed at it" Failure in meditation has occurred because persons may have gone into the practice with the wrong idea about what it is or with the wrong attitude in what they want from it. If your need for meditation is only what you can get out of it, you may have a selfish need. Meditation is more than that. So before you start your practice, let's talk about what meditation is not.

Click Here To Read The Rest Of
Meditation For Beginners: How To Meditate For Lifelong Peace, Focus and Happiness

P.S. You'll find many more books like this and others under my name Michele Gilbert.

Don't miss them... here is a short list.

Wicca: The Ultimate Beginners Guide For Witches and Warlocks: Learn Wicca Magic

The Introvert's Advantage: The Introverts Guide To Succeeding In An Extrovert World

Stop Playing Mind Games: How To Free Yourself Of Controlling And Manipulating Relationships

Instant Charisma: A Quick And Easy Guide To Talk, Impress, And Make Anyone Like You

Chakras: Understanding The 7 Main Chakras For Beginners: The Ultimate Guide To Chakra Mindfulness, Balance and Healing

Practicing Mindfulness: Living in the moment through Meditation: Everyday Habits and Rituals to help you achieve inner peace

Adrenal Fatigue: What Is Adrenal Fatigue Syndrome And How To Reset Your Diet And Your Life

Sleep Tight: Overcome Insomnia and Sleep Disorders for a better more restful sleep!

Stop Back Pain Now!: Back Pain Remedies and Treatments so you can live a pain free life!

The Arthritis Pain Cure: How to find Arthritis Pain Relief and live a happy pain free life!

The Headache Pain Cure: How to find Headache Pain Relief and live a happy Pain Free Life!

Stop Panic Attacks and Anxiety Disorders without Drugs Now!: Overcome Panic, Stress and Anxiety and live a happy pain free life!

The Breakup Recovery Guide: Advice for Surviving Heartbreak, Letting Go and Thriving in an exciting new life!

The Friendship Guide to Finding Friends Forever: How to Find, Make and Keep Quality Friendships After your Breakup

How To Stop Being Jealous And Insecure: Overcome Insecurity And Relationship Jealousy

Psychic Development: Your Guide To Unlocking Your Psychic Abilities

So I Am Dating A Psycopath: Now What?

The Mind Of A Sociopath: Your Guide to Understanding The Anti-Social Personality Disorder of Sociopaths

About Michele

Michele Gilbert was born and raised in Brooklyn, New York. Drawn to literature and writing at a young age, she enrolled at Brooklyn College and majored in English. After graduation Michele did not begin writing immediately, instead she embarked on a career in the finance industry and spent the next thirty years on Wall Street.

Serendipity struck when she least expected it. After ending a long-term relationship, Michele found herself lost and unsure what the future held. She began to read books on grief and loss, looking for answers. Those led her to delve deeper into the Law of Attraction and its power. What resulted was remarkable. Not only had she begun to heal, she had also rekindled her former love of writing and discovered her life's purpose.

The years have taken her through many twists and turns, but she learned valuable lessons along the way. Today she publishes books-mostly self-help and metaphysical in nature-and feels compelled to share her knowledge with those facing similar experiences. Her greatest hope is to inspire others and show them ways to overcome adversity and gracefully accept life's inevitable low points.

Going forward, she plans to incorporate more teachings of self-help, finance and meditation. Regular meditation is very beneficial to her progress as she forges a new life. Morning rituals and positive incantations are other practices Michele embraces; they are very restorative in daily life.

As an avid hiker, Michele and fellow club members often hike the picturesque Jersey Pine Barrens. She is a history buff, voracious reader, baseball fanatic and a foodie. She also proudly supports Trout Unlimited-a national non-profit organization dedicated to conserving, protecting and restoring North America's Coldwater fisheries and their watersheds.

Michele currently resides forty minutes from Atlantic City and the Jersey Shore. She makes her home with a Blue Russian rescue cat named Jersey, though she isn't exactly sure who rescued who.

Michele really enjoys publishing books that can make a difference in people's lives. If you have any suggestions or would like to have a specific topic covered in a future book, please send an email to michelegilbertbooks@gmail.com and we will get back to you.

Thanks for reading!

Recommended Additional Reading..

[No Excuses!: The Power of Self-Discipline](#)

[The Slight Edge: Turning Simple Disciplines into Massive Success and Happiness](#)

[The Willpower Instinct: How Self-Control Works, Why It Matters, and What You Can Do to Get More of It](#)

[Body Language 101: What A Person's Body Language Is Really Telling You...And How You Can Use It To Your Advantage](#)

[Buddhism For The Ultimate Seeker: Understanding Buddhism And The Buddhism Way Of Life](#)